NO CODE 101:
270 TOOLS TO BUILD WEBSITES, APPS AND SOFTWARE WITHOUT WRITING A SINGLE LINE OF CODE

2nd Edition

NO CODE 101: 270 TOOLS TO BUILD WEBSITES, APPS AND SOFTWARE WITHOUT WRITING A SINGLE LINE OF CODE

2nd Edition

LX VOLITION

LX VOLITION

NO CODE 101 - 2nd EDITION:
270 TOOLS TO BUILD WEBSITES, APPS AND SOFTWARE WITHOUT WRITING A SINGLE LINE OF CODE

ISBN-13: 978-9-99-879331-6

Copyright © 2022 Sven Marage
Copyright © 2022 LX Volition

Published by Sven Marage - LX Volition
Cover design by Sven Marage

Notice of rights
All rights reserved worldwide. No part of this publication may be reproduced or transmitted without the prior written consent of the publisher.

Disclaimer
The publisher is providing this book and its contents on an "as is" basis and makes no representations or warranties of any kind with respect to this book or its contents. The publisher and the author disclaim all such representations and warranties, including but not limited to warranties of healthcare for a particular purpose. In addition, the publisher and the author assume no responsibility for errors, inaccuracies, omissions, or any other inconsistencies herein.

lxvolition.com

No Code is Great.

Table of contents

Introduction — 1
    About No code — 1
    Who is this book for? — 1
    The structure — 2
    Additional resources — 3

Methodology — 5
    Order — 5
    Name — 5
    Description — 5
    Create — 5
    Free plan — 6
    Paid plan — 6
    Model — 6
    Works on top of… — 7
    Difficulty — 7
    Website URL — 8

Tools — 9

Index — 287

Additional resources — 289

Introduction

About No code

No code is a type of development which allows both people with and without programming knowledge to create software, websites and apps in a visual and graphic user interface.

No code is an ever growing market that attracts more and more "no-coders" every year. Indeed, it is the only way developers who do not know how to code can create their own digital products, while experienced programmers also benefit from this simplicity.

Please note that this book does not include low code tools. But what is the difference between no code and low code? Low code means that there is only a small part of code to insert in your development, which eases the task for programmers.

Who is this book for?

This book is for people who do not know how to code and want to create their own website, app, or piece of software.

In this book, you will find 270 no code tools that will allow you to create great products without writing a single line of code.

With these tools, you will be able to create AI tools, authentication & ID verification systems, automations, APIs, blogs, booking platforms, calculators, charts, maps, chatbots, classified ads, communities, forums, databases, documentation, directories, forms, internal apps, job boards, landing pages, personal pages, marketplaces, memberships, subscriptions, messaging apps, mobile apps, online stores, payments pages, pricing pages, prototypes, search engines, on-premises software, SaaS, streaming platforms, courses and e-learning platforms, testimonial pages, translations, video games, virtual events, virtual spaces, voting platforms, website activity trackers, and of course websites, all of this without code!

The structure

In the next chapter, *Methodology*, you will find more details about the classification of the tools in the third chapter, the categories (what kind of tools you can create), the descriptions, the fees, the difficulty and the requirements.

In the third part, the *Tools* chapter with one tool per page - or more if the categories or the descriptions are longer. Each page includes the URLs of the websites for you to access the tools more easily.

Additional resources

At the end of this book, you can find additional resources that will help you in creating your first - or next - tool, without code.

Also included is a QR code, which redirects to an Airtable table where you can find all the no code tools listed in this book.

Methodology

The aim of this chapter is to describe the structure of the *Tools* chapter. There are two types of classification: the order and the categories/details of each tool.

Order

The order is a mix of popularity, categories, functionalities and reliability. This information comes from search engines rankings, no code tools list, no code communities and ratings.

Name

The name is simply the name of the tool. It is the first piece of information about the tool listed on the tool page.

Description

The description of the tool can be two different things; it is either the title of the tool's website or web page, or the slogan the publisher used to describe the tool. The selection has been made in accordance with their pertinence.

Create

This category references every type of product you can create with this tool: mobile apps, websites, landing pages, memberships, messaging apps, and more. The emoji is present to illustrate the content.

To more easily find the tools that allow you to create a specific type of product, access the Index at the end of this book.

Notes: Only Website Activity Trackers that do not use cookies and are privacy-friendly appear in this book. Also includes tools with a clear and available pricing structure (no quoting).

Free plan
Is there a free plan available for this tool? If yes, "Yes"; if not, "-". Please note that a free trial is not a free plan.

Paid plan
How much does the cheapest plan cost for that tool? The reference of the fee is made according to the period stated on the website of the tool. Note that the fee appears with the currency defined by the tool's maker/publisher.

Model
The model represents the business model used by the tool publisher. There are four types of models:

- *Subscription:* You pay a monthly/yearly fee to access and use the tool.
- *One-time payment:* You only need to pay once to use the tool. Own it forever.
- *Transaction-based:* The fee depends on the amount of transactions performed through the platform you created using the no code tool - generally online stores and marketplaces. The no code platform retains a percentage of these transfers.
- *Pay-as-you-go:* Depending on the usage you have of this specific tool, you will pay a lower or higher fee.

Note: Free tools appear with a tag of each model.

Works on top of...

This means there is/are (an)other tool(s) that is/are complementary with this specific tool. For example, a website builder that needs an external database to function will require database tools such as Google Sheets or Airtable.

If you see more than one tool, it does not mean you need every tool listed to function, but one of them.

Difficulty

Two levels of difficulty exist:

- *"Simple - Little learning required"*

- *"I am willing to learn"*

These levels of difficulty indicate how much knowledge you have to acquire to use the tool, and the level of learning required to get started.

Website URL

The website URL is the address you have to input in the search bar to access the website or the web page of the tool.

Tools

Name
Bubble

Description
The best way to build web apps without code

Create
Mobile Apps 📱, Classified Ads 📰, Memberships & Subscriptions 💳, Online Stores 🛍, Prototypes 🔧, Virtual Events 🎪, Websites 🌐, Messaging Apps 💬, Marketplaces 🛒, Communities & Forums 🗣, Software (Online/SaaS) 💻, Voting Platforms 🗳, Job Boards 💼, Booking Platforms 📖, Internal Apps & Client Portals 📁, Streaming & Courses Platforms 🎬

Free plan
Yes

Paid plan
From $25/month

Model
Subscription

Works on top of
-

Difficulty
I am willing to learn

Website URL
https://bubble.io/

Name
Airtable

Description
Customize your workflow, collaborate, and achieve ambitious outcomes

Create
Databases 📁

Free plan
Yes

Paid plan
From $10/month

Model
Subscription

Works on top of
-

Difficulty
Simple - Little learning required, I am willing to learn

Website URL
https://airtable.com/

Name
Notion

Description
All-in-one workspace

Create
Documentation & Guides 📚, Blogs 📓

Free plan
Yes

Paid plan
From $4/month

Model
Subscription

Works on top of
-

Difficulty
Simple - Little learning required, I am willing to learn

Website URL
https://www.notion.so/

Name
Glide

Description
Build an app from a Google Sheet in five minutes, for free

Create
Mobile Apps 📱, Software (Online/SaaS) 💻

Free plan
Yes

Paid plan
From $32/month

Model
Subscription

Works on top of
Needs Google Sheets, Needs Microsoft Excel

Difficulty
Simple - Little learning required, I am willing to learn

Website URL
https://www.glideapps.com/

Name
AppGyver

Description
You will never go back to coding. Seriously.

Create
Mobile Apps 📱

Free plan
Yes

Paid plan
Free until $10M revenue

Model
One-time payment, Subscription, Transaction-based, Pay-as-you-go

Works on top of
-

Difficulty
I am willing to learn

Website URL
https://www.appgyver.com/

Name
Softr

Description
The easiest way to build from Airtable

Create
Classified Ads 🟫, Directories 📌, Memberships & Subscriptions 🎞️, Software (Online/SaaS) 💼, Websites ⚫, Marketplaces 🐱, Voting Platforms ⬢, Job Boards 💼

Free plan
Yes

Paid plan
From $24/month

Model
Subscription

Works on top of
Needs Airtable

Difficulty
Simple - Little learning required, I am willing to learn

Website URL
https://www.softr.io/

Name
Carrd

Description
Simple, free, fully responsive one-page sites for pretty much anything

Create
Landing & Personal Pages 🔗, Websites ⚫

Free plan
Yes

Paid plan
From $19/year

Model
Subscription

Works on top of
-

Difficulty
Simple - Little learning required, I am willing to learn

Website URL
https://carrd.co

Name
Webflow

Description
The modern way to build for the web

Create
Websites ●, Online Stores ⬢

Free plan
Yes

Paid plan
From $12/month

Model
Subscription

Works on top of
-

Difficulty
I am willing to learn

Website URL
https://webflow.com/

Name
Pricewell

Description
Build Stripe subscriptions into your website in minutes

Create
Pricing Pages 💲

Free plan
Yes

Paid plan
Free up to $10k MRR

Model
One-time payment, Subscription, Transaction-based, Pay-as-you-go

Works on top of
Needs Stripe

Difficulty
Simple - Little learning required, I am willing to learn

Website URL
https://www.pricewell.io/

Name
Plausible

Description
Simple and privacy-friendly Google Analytics alternative

Create
Website Activity Trackers

Free plan
-

Paid plan
From €6/month

Model
Subscription

Works on top of
-

Difficulty
Simple - Little learning required, I am willing to learn

Website URL
https://plausible.io/

Name
Simple Analytics

Description
Simple, clean, and privacy-friendly analytics

Create
Website Activity Trackers

Free plan
-

Paid plan
From €19/month

Model
Subscription

Works on top of
-

Difficulty
Simple - Little learning required, I am willing to learn

Website URL
https://simpleanalytics.com/

Name
Super

Description
Build simple websites with nothing but Notion

Create
Websites ●

Free plan
-

Paid plan
$12/month

Model
Subscription

Works on top of
Needs Notion

Difficulty
Simple - Little learning required, I am willing to learn

Website URL
https://super.so/

Name
Fathom

Description
Simple & private analytics for bloggers & businesses

Create
Website Activity Trackers

Free plan
-

Paid plan
From $14/month

Model
Subscription

Works on top of
-

Difficulty
Simple - Little learning required, I am willing to learn

Website URL
https://usefathom.com/

Name
Bildr

Description
Build beautiful, complete SaaS products.

Create
Mobile Apps 📱, Software (Online/SaaS) 💻, Internal Apps & Client Portals 💼

Free plan
Yes

Paid plan
From $9/month

Model
Subscription

Works on top of
-

Difficulty
I am willing to learn

Website URL
https://www.bildr.com/

Name
Zapier

Description
Connect your apps and automate workflows

Create
Automations & APIs

Free plan
Yes

Paid plan
From $19.99/month

Model
Subscription

Works on top of
-

Difficulty
I am willing to learn

Website URL
https://zapier.com/

Name
Make

Description
Make lets you design, build, and automate anything - from tasks and workflows to apps and systems - in a few clicks

Create
Automations & APIs

Free plan
Yes

Paid plan
From $9/month

Model
Subscription

Works on top of
-

Difficulty
I am willing to learn

Website URL
https://www.make.com/en

Name
Automate.io

Description
Connect your cloud apps. Automate work.

Create
Automations & APIs

Free plan
Yes

Paid plan
From $9.99/month

Model
Subscription

Works on top of
-

Difficulty
I am willing to learn

Website URL
https://automate.io/

Name
n8n

Description
Free and open workflow automation tool

Create
Automations & APIs

Free plan
Yes

Paid plan
From €20/month

Model
Subscription

Works on top of
-

Difficulty
I am willing to learn

Website URL
https://n8n.io/

Name
NoCodeAPI

Description
Build third-party application APIs

Create
Automations & APIs

Free plan
Yes

Paid plan
From $6/month

Model
Subscription

Works on top of
-

Difficulty
I am willing to learn

Website URL
https://nocodeapi.com/

Name
Data Fetcher

Description
Connect Airtable to any API

Create
Automations & APIs

Free plan
Yes

Paid plan
From $18/month

Model
Subscription

Works on top of
Needs Airtable

Difficulty
I am willing to learn

Website URL
https://datafetcher.com/

Name
Stripe Checkout

Description
The quickest way to build conversion-optimized payment forms, hosted on Stripe.

Create
Payment Pages

Free plan

Paid plan
From 1.4% + 0.3%

Model
Transaction-based

Works on top of
-

Difficulty
I am willing to learn

Website URL
https://stripe.com/docs/payments/checkout

Name
PayPal Checkout

Description
Offer more payment options to your customers

Create
Payment Pages 💳

Free plan
-

Paid plan
From 3.49%

Model
Transaction-based

Works on top of
-

Difficulty
I am willing to learn

Website URL
https://www.paypal.com/us/webapps/mpp/paypal-checkout

Name
WordPress.com

Description
WordPress.com is a platform for self-publishing that is popular for blogging and other works

Create
Websites ●, Blogs ▮, Landing & Personal Pages 🖇, Online Stores ⬢

Free plan
Yes

Paid plan
From €4/month

Model
Subscription

Works on top of
-

Difficulty
Simple - Little learning required, I am willing to learn

Website URL
https://wordpress.com/

Name
WordPress.org

Description
WordPress is open source software you can use to create a beautiful website, blog, or app

Create
Websites ●, Blogs ▐, Classified Ads ▮, Directories ⚲, Marketplaces ☗, Memberships & Subscriptions ▬, Online Stores ●, Software (Online/SaaS) ▮, Communities & Forums ☙, Internal Apps & Client Portals ▮, Job Boards ▣, Search Engines & Tools ⚲, Voting Platforms ●, Streaming & Courses Platforms ▮, Messaging Apps ●

Free plan
Yes

Paid plan
Free

Model
One-time payment, Subscription, Transaction-based, Pay-as-you-go

Works on top of
-

Difficulty
I am willing to learn

Website URL
https://wordpress.org/

Name
Adalo

Description
Turn your idea into reality without coding

Create
Mobile Apps 📱

Free plan
Yes

Paid plan
From $50/month

Model
Subscription

Works on top of
-

Difficulty
I am willing to learn

Website URL
https://www.adalo.com/

Name
Memberstack

Description
Beautiful user logins & payments for any website

Create
Memberships & Subscriptions 🎟, Payment Pages 💳, Authentication & ID Verification 🔐, Automations & APIs 🧩

Free plan
-

Paid plan
From $25/month + 3% transaction fees

Model
Subscription, Transaction-based

Works on top of
-

Difficulty
I am willing to learn

Website URL
https://www.memberstack.com/

Name
Appy Pie

Description
#1 No code development platform

Create
Mobile Apps 📱 , Websites 🌐, Automations & APIs 🔗

Free plan
-

Paid plan
From $9.99/month

Model
Subscription

Works on top of
-

Difficulty
I am willing to learn

Website URL
https://www.appypie.com/

Name
Gumroad

Description
Creators deserve to get paid for their work. Gumroad makes it easy.

Create
Memberships & Subscriptions 🎬, Online Stores ⬢, Payment Pages 💳

Free plan
-

Paid plan
From 7.5% transaction fees

Model
Transaction-based

Works on top of
-

Difficulty
Simple - Little learning required, I am willing to learn

Website URL
https://gumroad.com/

Name
Weglot

Description
Weglot allows you to make your website multilingual in minutes

Create
Translations 🟫

Free plan
-

Paid plan
From $99/year

Model
Subscription

Works on top of
-

Difficulty
Simple - Little learning required, I am willing to learn

Website URL
https://weglot.com/

Name
Tally

Description
The simplest way to create forms

Create
Forms ?

Free plan
Yes

Paid plan
From $25/month

Model
Subscription

Works on top of
-

Difficulty
Simple - Little learning required, I am willing to learn

Website URL
https://tally.so/

Name
Typeform

Description
Create forms and surveys that people enjoy answering

Create
Forms ?

Free plan
-

Paid plan
From €18/month

Model
Subscription

Works on top of
-

Difficulty
Simple - Little learning required, I am willing to learn

Website URL
https://www.typeform.com/

Name
Google Sheets

Description
With Google Sheets, you can create, edit, and collaborate wherever you are

Create
Databases 📁

Free plan
Yes

Paid plan
Free

Model
One-time payment, Subscription, Transaction-based, Pay-as-you-go

Works on top of
-

Difficulty
Simple - Little learning required, I am willing to learn

Website URL
https://docs.google.com/

Name
Thunkable

Description
We make it easy to build your best apps

Create
Mobile Apps 📱, Prototypes 💪

Free plan
Yes

Paid plan
From $13/month

Model
Subscription

Works on top of
-

Difficulty
I am willing to learn

Website URL
https://thunkable.com/

Name
Chilipepper

Description
Create beautiful forms connected to your Notion pages

Create
Forms ?

Free plan
Yes

Paid plan
$5/month

Model
Subscription

Works on top of
Needs Notion

Difficulty
Simple - Little learning required, I am willing to learn

Website URL
https://chilipepper.io/

Name
Appsheet

Description
Reclaim your time and talent with no-code apps and automation

Create
Internal Apps & Client Portals 💼

Free plan
Yes

Paid plan
From $5/month

Model
Subscription

Works on top of
-

Difficulty
Simple - Little learning required, I am willing to learn

Website URL
https://www.appsheet.com/

Name
Figma

Description
Figma connects everyone in the design process so teams can deliver better products, faster

Create
Prototypes 💪

Free plan
Yes

Paid plan
From $12/month

Model
Subscription

Works on top of
-

Difficulty
Simple - Little learning required, I am willing to learn

Website URL
https://www.figma.com/

Name
Bravo Studio

Description
The fastest tool to build better prototypes, validate ideas and launch real products

Create
Mobile Apps 📱, Prototypes 💪

Free plan
Yes

Paid plan
From €19/month

Model
Subscription

Works on top of
-

Difficulty
Simple - Little learning required, I am willing to learn

Website URL
https://www.bravostudio.app/

Name
Canva

Description
Create beautiful designs with your team

Create
Other useful tools

Free plan
Yes

Paid plan
From $119.99/year

Model
Subscription

Works on top of
-

Difficulty
Simple - Little learning required, I am willing to learn

Website URL
https://www.canva.com/

Name
Bannerbear

Description
Auto-generate social media visuals, ecommerce banners, dynamic email images and more

Create
Other useful tools 💡

Free plan
-

Paid plan
From $49/month

Model
Subscription

Works on top of
-

Difficulty
Simple - Little learning required, I am willing to learn

Website URL
https://www.bannerbear.com/

Name
LunaPic

Description
Completely free online photo editing

Create
Other useful tools

Free plan
Yes

Paid plan
Free

Model
One-time payment, Subscription, Transaction-based, Pay-as-you-go

Works on top of
-

Difficulty
Simple - Little learning required, I am willing to learn

Website URL
https://www9.lunapic.com/

Name
Active FYI

Description
Let your users know that your product is active & supported

Create
Other useful tools

Free plan
-

Paid plan
From $2.50/month

Model
Subscription

Works on top of
-

Difficulty
Simple - Little learning required, I am willing to learn

Website URL
https://active.fyi

Name
Duffel

Description
Start selling flights online today

Create
Automations & APIs 📕, *Other useful tools* 💡, Booking Platforms 📓

Free plan
-

Paid plan
Depends

Model
One-time payment, Subscription, Transaction-based, Pay-as-you-go

Works on top of
-

Difficulty
I am willing to learn

Website URL
https://duffel.com/

Name
Octane AI

Description
Everything you need to increase sales on Shopify with quizzes

Create
Other useful tools

Free plan
-

Paid plan
From $29/month

Model
Subscription

Works on top of
Needs Shopify

Difficulty
I am willing to learn

Website URL
https://www.octaneai.com/

Name
Yeah, Pics!

Description
Find all the best free-usable images and pictures, at a glance

Create
Other useful tools

Free plan
Yes

Paid plan
Free

Model
One-time payment, Subscription, Transaction-based, Pay-as-you-go

Works on top of
-

Difficulty
Simple - Little learning required, I am willing to learn

Website URL
https://yeah.pics

Name
Google Forms

Description
Create a new survey and edit it with others at the same time

Create
Forms ?

Free plan
Yes

Paid plan
Free

Model
One-time payment, Subscription, Transaction-based, Pay-as-you-go

Works on top of
-

Difficulty
Simple - Little learning required, I am willing to learn

Website URL
https://www.google.com/forms/about/

Name
Mixily

Description
Everything you need to host virtual events for your community

Create
Virtual Spaces 🎡

Free plan
Yes

Paid plan
From $30/month

Model
Subscription

Works on top of
-

Difficulty
Simple - Little learning required, I am willing to learn

Website URL
https://www.mixily.com/

Name
Shopify

Description
The platform commerce is built on

Create
Online Stores

Free plan
-

Paid plan
From $9/month

Model
Subscription

Works on top of
-

Difficulty
Simple - Little learning required, I am willing to learn

Website URL
https://www.shopify.com/

Name
Ecwid

Description
Your free online store is just a few clicks away

Create
Online Stores

Free plan
Yes

Paid plan
From €12.50/month

Model
Subscription

Works on top of
-

Difficulty
Simple - Little learning required, I am willing to learn

Website URL
https://www.ecwid.com

Name
involve.me

Description
Create personalized interactions at every step of the customer journey

Create
Forms ?

Free plan
Yes

Paid plan
From $19/month

Model
Subscription

Works on top of
-

Difficulty
Simple - Little learning required, I am willing to learn

Website URL
https://www.involve.me/

Name
Mollie

Description
Start growing your business with effortless payments

Create
Payment Pages

Free plan
-

Paid plan
From €0.10 per transaction

Model
Transaction-based

Works on top of
-

Difficulty
Simple - Little learning required, I am willing to learn

Website URL
https://www.mollie.com/

Name
Dorik

Description
Flexible & easy-to-use nocode website builder with 130+ UI Components and beautiful templates

Create
Websites 🌑, Landing & Personal Pages 📎

Free plan
Yes

Paid plan
From $3/month

Model
Subscription

Works on top of
-

Difficulty
Simple - Little learning required, I am willing to learn

Website URL
https://dorik.com/

Name
Chargebee

Description
Chargebee is the subscription billing and revenue management platform that lets you solve for your today, and scale for your tomorrow

Create
Payment Pages 🖼️

Free plan
Yes

Paid plan
From $249/month

Model
Subscription

Works on top of
-

Difficulty
Simple - Little learning required, I am willing to learn

Website URL
https://www.chargebee.com/

Name
Ghost

Description
Turn your audience into a business

Create
Blogs 📓

Free plan
-

Paid plan
From $9/month

Model
Subscription

Works on top of
-

Difficulty
Simple - Little learning required, I am willing to learn

Website URL
https://ghost.org/

Name
JotForm

Description
Powerful forms that use conditional logic, accept payments and generate reports

Create
Forms ?

Free plan
Yes

Paid plan
From $24/month

Model
Subscription

Works on top of
-

Difficulty
Simple - Little learning required, I am willing to learn

Website URL
https://www.jotform.com/

Name
SurveyMonkey

Description
Talk to the people who matter to you

Create
Forms ?

Free plan
Yes

Paid plan
From €30/month

Model
Subscription

Works on top of
-

Difficulty
Simple - Little learning required, I am willing to learn

Website URL
https://www.surveymonkey.com/

Name
Testimonial.io

Description
Get video testimonials from your customers with ease

Create
Testimonial Pages 🖤

Free plan
Yes

Paid plan
From $50/month

Model
Subscription

Works on top of
-

Difficulty
Simple - Little learning required, I am willing to learn

Website URL
https://testimonial.to/

Name
Medium

Description
Medium is a place to write, read, and connect

Create
Blogs 📓

Free plan
Yes

Paid plan
Free

Model
One-time payment, Subscription, Transaction-based, Pay-as-you-go

Works on top of
-

Difficulty
Simple - Little learning required, I am willing to learn

Website URL
https://medium.com/

Name
Mangools SERP Simulator

Description
Google SERP Simulator

Create
Other useful tools

Free plan
Yes

Paid plan
Free

Model
One-time payment, Subscription, Transaction-based, Pay-as-you-go

Works on top of
-

Difficulty
Simple - Little learning required, I am willing to learn

Website URL
https://mangools.com/free-seo-tools/serp-simulator

Name
Jitter

Description
Motion design, made simple

Create
Other useful tools

Free plan
Yes

Paid plan
$9/month

Model
Subscription

Works on top of
-

Difficulty
Simple - Little learning required, I am willing to learn

Website URL
https://jitter.video/

Name
Logiak

Description
Slash development times and maintenance costs, and have full control over system development

Create
Mobile Apps 📱, Internal Apps & Client Portals 💼

Free plan
-

Paid plan
From $500/month

Model
Subscription

Works on top of
-

Difficulty
Simple - Little learning required, I am willing to learn

Website URL
https://www.logiak.com/

Name
Wix

Description
Discover the platform that gives you the freedom to create, design, manage and develop your web presence

Create
Websites ⬢, Online Stores ⬢, Landing & Personal Pages 📎, Blogs 📕

Free plan
Yes

Paid plan
From €4.50/month

Model
Subscription

Works on top of
-

Difficulty
Simple - Little learning required, I am willing to learn

Website URL

https://wix.com

Name
Blogger

Description
Create a unique and beautiful blog. It's easy and free.

Create
Blogs 📓

Free plan
Yes

Paid plan
Free

Model
One-time payment, Subscription, Transaction-based, Pay-as-you-go

Works on top of
-

Difficulty
Simple - Little learning required, I am willing to learn

Website URL
https://www.blogger.com/

Name
Tumblr

Description
Tumblr is a place to express yourself, discover yourself, and bond over the stuff you love

Create
Blogs 📔

Free plan
Yes

Paid plan
Free

Model
One-time payment, Subscription, Transaction-based, Pay-as-you-go

Works on top of

Difficulty
Simple - Little learning required, I am willing to learn

Website URL
https://www.tumblr.com/

Name
Typedream

Description
Everything you need to build your website in record time

Create
Websites

Free plan
Yes

Paid plan
$12/month

Model
Subscription

Works on top of
-

Difficulty
Simple - Little learning required, I am willing to learn

Website URL
https://typedream.com/

Name
Squarespace

Description
Everything to sell anything

Create
Websites 🟢, Landing & Personal Pages 📎, Online Stores ⬢, Blogs 📕, Memberships & Subscriptions 🎞️

Free plan
-

Paid plan
From $12/month

Model
Subscription

Works on top of
-

Difficulty
Simple - Little learning required, I am willing to learn

Website URL
https://squarespace.com/

Name
Buy Me a Coffee

Description
Buy Me a Coffee is a simple, meaningful way to fund your creative work

Create
Memberships & Subscriptions

Free plan
-

Paid plan
5% transaction fee

Model
Transaction-based

Works on top of
-

Difficulty
Simple - Little learning required, I am willing to learn

Website URL
https://www.buymeacoffee.com/

Name
Patreon

Description
Let your most passionate fans support your creative work via monthly membership

Create
Memberships & Subscriptions 🎬

Free plan
-

Paid plan
From 5% transaction fee

Model
Transaction-based

Works on top of
-

Difficulty
Simple - Little learning required, I am willing to learn

Website URL
https://www.patreon.com/

Name
Ko-Fi

Description
The free, friendly way to accept donations, memberships and sales directly from fans

Create
Memberships & Subscriptions

Free plan
Yes

Paid plan
5% transaction fee

Model
Transaction-based

Works on top of
-

Difficulty
Simple - Little learning required, I am willing to learn

Website URL
https://ko-fi.com/

Name
Moqups

Description
A streamlined web app that helps you create and collaborate in real-time on wireframes, mockups, diagrams and prototypes

Create
Prototypes 💪

Free plan
Yes

Paid plan
From €13/month

Model
Subscription

Works on top of
-

Difficulty
Simple - Little learning required, I am willing to learn

Website URL
https://moqups.com/

Name
Proto.io

Description
The prototyping solution for all your needs

Create
Prototypes 💪

Free plan
-

Paid plan
From $24/month

Model
Subscription

Works on top of
-

Difficulty
Simple - Little learning required, I am willing to learn

Website URL
https://proto.io/

Name
Marvel

Description
Rapid prototyping, testing and handoff for modern design teams

Create
Prototypes 💪

Free plan
Yes

Paid plan
From $12/month

Model
Subscription

Works on top of
-

Difficulty
Simple - Little learning required, I am willing to learn

Website URL
https://marvelapp.com/

Name
Justinmind

Description
Design and prototyping tool for web and mobile apps

Create
Prototypes 💪

Free plan
Yes

Paid plan
From $9/month

Model
Subscription

Works on top of
-

Difficulty
Simple - Little learning required, I am willing to learn

Website URL
https://www.justinmind.com/

Name
Umso

Description
We automatically generate unique websites based on your usecase

Create
Websites 🌐

Free plan
-

Paid plan
From $25/month

Model
Subscription

Works on top of
-

Difficulty
Simple - Little learning required, I am willing to learn

Website URL
https://www.umso.com/

Name
Elliott

Description
Instantly sell & ship to 200+ countries, zero introductory fees

Create
Online Stores

Free plan
Yes

Paid plan
2.9% + $0.30

Model
Transaction-based

Works on top of
-

Difficulty
Simple - Little learning required, I am willing to learn

Website URL
https://elliot.store/

Name
Edit

Description
Live modify any web page directly from your browser, with a single click

Create
Prototypes 💪, *Other useful tools* 💡

Free plan
-

Paid plan
From $15

Model
One-time payment

Works on top of
Needs Google Chrome

Difficulty
Simple - Little learning required, I am willing to learn

Website URL
https://goedit.me/

Name
Appeggio

Description
You get a Website, iPhone and Android apps all from the one effort

Create
Mobile Apps 📱, Websites ⬤, Landing & Personal Pages 📎

Free plan
-

Paid plan
$50/month

Model
Subscription

Works on top of
-

Difficulty
Simple - Little learning required, I am willing to learn

Website URL
https://appeggio.com/

Name
Duda

Description
The professional website builder you can call your own

Create
Websites 🔴

Free plan
-

Paid plan
From $14/month

Model
Subscription

Works on top of
-

Difficulty
Simple - Little learning required, I am willing to learn

Website URL
https://www.duda.co/

Name
Ycode

Description
Visually build and design beautiful, responsive web projects without compromising your vision

Create
Websites 🔴, Software (Online/SaaS) 🔨, Classified Ads 💼, Directories 📌, Internal Apps & Client Portals 💼, Marketplaces 🥟, Job Boards 💼

Free plan
Yes

Paid plan
From $39/month

Model
Subscription

Works on top of
-

Difficulty
Simple - Little learning required, I am willing to learn

Website URL
https://www.ycode.com/

Name
Tilda Publishing

Description
Create beautiful websites without any code

Create
Online Stores ⬢, Websites ●

Free plan
Yes

Paid plan
From $10/month

Model
Subscription

Works on top of
-

Difficulty
Simple - Little learning required, I am willing to learn

Website URL
https://tilda.cc/

Name
Cantrip

Description
The easiest website builder you will ever use

Create
Websites ⬤

Free plan
Yes

Paid plan
$9.98/month

Model
Subscription

Works on top of
-

Difficulty
Simple - Little learning required, I am willing to learn

Website URL
https://cantrip.io/

Name
Pazly

Description
Great landing pages for small businesses

Create
Landing & Personal Pages 📎

Free plan
Yes

Paid plan
$5.99/month

Model
Subscription

Works on top of
-

Difficulty
Simple - Little learning required, I am willing to learn

Website URL
https://pazly.dev/

Name
Passbase

Description
Securely verify customers' identities through ID documents, selfies, and government databases

Create
Authentication & ID Verification

Free plan
-

Paid plan
$1.49/verification

Model
Pay-as-you-go

Works on top of
-

Difficulty
I am willing to learn

Website URL
https://passbase.com/

Name
Solidpixels

Description
The direct path to a world-class website

Create
Landing & Personal Pages 🔗, Online Stores ⬢, Websites ●

Free plan

Paid plan
From €21/month

Model
Subscription

Works on top of
-

Difficulty
Simple - Little learning required, I am willing to learn

Website URL
https://www.solidpixels.com/en

Name
Quest AI

Description
Convert your design into a launch ready website

Create
Prototypes 💪, Websites ⚫

Free plan
Yes

Paid plan
From $15/month

Model
Subscription

Works on top of
-

Difficulty
Simple - Little learning required, I am willing to learn

Website URL
https://www.quest.ai/

Name
Directual

Description
Power of coding in no-code format

Create
Internal Apps & Client Portals 💼

Free plan
Yes

Paid plan
From $29/month

Model
Subscription

Works on top of
-

Difficulty
I am willing to learn

Website URL
https://www.directual.com/

Name
Berta

Description
A simple way to make your own website

Create
Landing & Personal Pages 📎, Websites ⚫

Free plan
-

Paid plan
From €3.99/month

Model
Subscription

Works on top of
-

Difficulty
Simple - Little learning required, I am willing to learn

Website URL
https://berta.me/

Name
Bloggi

Description
Create a blog in seconds

Create
Blogs 📓

Free plan
Yes

Paid plan
$9/month

Model
Subscription

Works on top of
-

Difficulty
Simple - Little learning required, I am willing to learn

Website URL
https://bloggi.co/

Name
Bookmark

Description
Let our AI powered website builder get your business online in minutes

Create
Online Stores ⬢, Websites ⬤

Free plan
Yes

Paid plan
From $11.99/month

Model
Subscription

Works on top of
-

Difficulty
Simple - Little learning required, I am willing to learn

Website URL
https://www.bookmark.com/

Name
IM Creator

Description
Personal & white label CMS

Create
Online Stores ⬢, Websites ●

Free plan
Yes

Paid plan
From $8/month

Model
Subscription

Works on top of
-

Difficulty
I am willing to learn

Website URL
https://www.imcreator.com/

Name
Jimdo

Description
Effortlessly create your professional website or store

Create
Blogs 🟫, Online Stores ⬣, Websites ⬤

Free plan
Yes

Paid plan
From $9/month

Model
Subscription

Works on top of
-

Difficulty
Simple - Little learning required, I am willing to learn

Website URL
https://www.jimdo.com/

Name
Paper Website

Description
Start a tiny website from your notebook

Create
Blogs 📓

Free plan
-

Paid plan
$10/month

Model
Subscription

Works on top of
-

Difficulty
Simple - Little learning required, I am willing to learn

Website URL
https://paperwebsite.com/

Name
Mobirise

Description
Create fast, mobile and high-ranking websites

Create
Landing & Personal Pages 📎, Websites ⚫

Free plan
Yes

Paid plan
Free

Model
One-time payment, Subscription, Transaction-based, Pay-as-you-go

Works on top of
-

Difficulty
Simple - Little learning required, I am willing to learn

Website URL
https://mobirise.com/

Name
Pixpa

Description
Easy & affordable way to build your website, portfolio, store & blog

Create
Online Stores ⬣, Websites ⬣

Free plan
-

Paid plan
From $7/month

Model
Subscription

Works on top of
-

Difficulty
Simple - Little learning required, I am willing to learn

Website URL
https://www.pixpa.com/

Name
Podia

Description
Sell courses, webinars, downloads, and memberships

Create
Memberships & Subscriptions 🎞️, Online Stores ⬢, Websites ⬤, Streaming & Courses Platforms 🎬

Free plan
-

Paid plan
From $39/month

Model
Subscription

Works on top of
-

Difficulty
Simple - Little learning required, I am willing to learn

Website URL
https://www.podia.com/

Name
Subbly

Description
Use Subbly to power your subscription business

Create
Memberships & Subscriptions

Free plan
-

Paid plan
From $14/month

Model
Subscription

Works on top of
-

Difficulty
Simple - Little learning required

Website URL
https://www.subbly.co/

Name
Readymag

Description
Landing pages, company websites, editorials, portfolios - the format doesn't matter, just design

Create
Landing & Personal Pages 📎, Websites ⬤

Free plan
Yes

Paid plan
From $15/month

Model
Subscription

Works on top of
-

Difficulty
Simple - Little learning required, I am willing to learn

Website URL
https://readymag.com/

Name
Sharetribe

Description
Build a successful marketplace business

Create
Marketplaces 🛡

Free plan
-

Paid plan
From $79/month

Model
Subscription

Works on top of
-

Difficulty
Simple - Little learning required, I am willing to learn

Website URL
https://www.sharetribe.com/

Name
Strinkingly

Description
Make a website in minutes

Create
Mobile Apps 📱, Online Stores ⬢, Websites ⬤

Free plan
Yes

Paid plan
From $8/month

Model
Subscription

Works on top of
-

Difficulty
Simple - Little learning required, I am willing to learn

Website URL
https://strikingly.com/

Name
Studio

Description
Turn ideas to live web experiences, in one place with your team

Create
Prototypes 💪, Websites ⚫

Free plan
-

Paid plan
From $9/month

Model
Subscription

Works on top of
-

Difficulty
Simple - Little learning required, I am willing to learn

Website URL
https://studio.design/

Name
Udesly

Description
Use Webflow to design your project and convert it in seconds with Udesly

Create
Forms ?, Online Stores ⬢, Websites ●

Free plan
Yes

Paid plan
From €14.56/month

Model
Subscription

Works on top of
Needs Google Chrome, Needs Webflow

Difficulty
Simple - Little learning required, I am willing to learn

Website URL
https://www.udesly.com/

Name
Versoly

Description
Build landing pages quickly

Create
Landing & Personal Pages 🔗

Free plan
Yes

Paid plan
From $19/month

Model
Subscription

Works on top of
-

Difficulty
I am willing to learn

Website URL
https://versoly.com/

Name
Weblium

Description
The most effortless
way to build

Create
Landing & Personal Pages 📎, Websites ⚫

Free plan
Yes

Paid plan
From $8.25/month

Model
Subscription

Works on top of
-

Difficulty
Simple - Little learning required, I am willing to learn

Website URL
https://weblium.com/

Name
Webnode

Description
Create an amazing website with Webnode in just minutes

Create
Blogs 🍞, Online Stores ⬢, Websites ⬤

Free plan
Yes

Paid plan
From $3.90/month

Model
Subscription

Works on top of
-

Difficulty
Simple - Little learning required, I am willing to learn

Website URL
https://us.webnode.com/

Name
Potion

Description
Create custom websites in minutes. All on Notion.

Create
Websites 🌐, Landing & Personal Pages 📎, Blogs 📓

Free plan
-

Paid plan
From $8/month

Model
Subscription

Works on top of
Needs Notion

Difficulty
Simple - Little learning required, I am willing to learn

Website URL
https://www.potion.so/

Name
Webydo

Description
The complete website builder & CMS for designers

Create
Websites ●

Free plan
-

Paid plan
From $75/month

Model
Subscription

Works on top of
-

Difficulty
Simple - Little learning required, I am willing to learn

Website URL
https://www.webydo.com/

Name
Sheet2Site

Description
Create your own website using only Google Sheets

Create
Online Stores 🔷, Websites ⚫, Directories 📌, Classified Ads 🟫, Voting Platforms ⬡, Job Boards 💼

Free plan
-

Paid plan
From $29/month

Model
Subscription

Works on top of
Needs Google Sheets

Difficulty
Simple - Little learning required, I am willing to learn

Website URL
https://www.sheet2site.com/

Name
Without Code

Description
Build faster websites, in half the time

Create
Online Stores ⬢, Websites ⬢

Free plan
Yes

Paid plan
From $99/year

Model
Subscription

Works on top of
-

Difficulty
Simple - Little learning required, I am willing to learn

Website URL
https://www.wocode.com/

Name
Presto API

Description
Build an API within minutes

Create
Automations & APIs

Free plan
Yes

Paid plan
From $49/month

Model
Subscription

Works on top of
-

Difficulty
I am willing to learn

Website URL
https://prestoapi.com/

Name
Calcapp

Description
Connect Excel-like formulas—with support for close to 300 functions—to the fields of your app

Create
Mobile Apps 📱, Calculators 🧮

Free plan
Yes

Paid plan
From $9/month

Model
Subscription

Works on top of
-

Difficulty
Simple - Little learning required, I am willing to learn

Website URL
https://www.calcapp.net/

Name
Zyllio

Description
Create mobile apps in minutes

Create
Mobile Apps 📱

Free plan
Yes

Paid plan
From $19/month

Model
Subscription

Works on top of
-

Difficulty
Simple - Little learning required, I am willing to learn

Website URL
https://zyllio.com/

Name
Pineapple

Description
Build apps. Using your phone, tablet or computer.

Create
Mobile Apps 📱

Free plan
-

Paid plan
$4.99/month

Model
Subscription

Works on top of
-

Difficulty
Simple - Little learning required, I am willing to learn

Website URL
https://pineapple.build/

Name
GitBook

Description
Publish beautiful docs for your users and centralize your teams' knowledge

Create
Documentation & Guides

Free plan
Yes

Paid plan
From $6.40/month

Model
Subscription

Works on top of
-

Difficulty
Simple - Little learning required, I am willing to learn

Website URL
https://www.gitbook.com/

Name
Pico

Description
Sell memberships, subscription paywalls, email collection, free and paid newsletters, online courses, digital downloads, donations, tipping & one time passes

Create
Memberships & Subscriptions 🎞

Free plan
Yes

Paid plan
From $5/month

Model
Subscription

Works on top of
Difficulty
Simple - Little learning required, I am willing to learn

Website URL
https://trypico.com/

Name
Newsy

Description
Turn your unused domain into a complete web application

Create
Other useful tools

Free plan
Yes

Paid plan
From $3/month

Model
Subscription

Works on top of
-

Difficulty
Simple - Little learning required, I am willing to learn

Website URL
https://www.newsy.co/

Name
Thorium Builder

Description
Create cross-platform Apps & Web Sites without technical skills

Create
Mobile Apps 📱, Websites 🌐

Free plan
Yes

Paid plan
From $89

Model
One-time payment

Works on top of
-

Difficulty
I am willing to learn

Website URL
https://www.thoriumbuilder.com/

Name
V.One

Description
The simplest app builder for beautifully simple apps

Create
Mobile Apps 📱

Free plan
-

Paid plan
From $8/month

Model
Subscription

Works on top of
-

Difficulty
Simple - Little learning required, I am willing to learn

Website URL
https://www.yourvone.com/

Name
AppInstitute

Description
Build mobile apps quickly without writing a single line of code

Create
Mobile Apps 📱

Free plan
-

Paid plan
From $59/month

Model
Subscription

Works on top of
-

Difficulty
Simple - Little learning required, I am willing to learn

Website URL
https://appinstitute.com/

Name
Sandbox Commerce

Description
Build beautiful, fully customizable mobile apps for your store

Create
Mobile Apps 📱 , Online Stores 🧊

Free plan
-

Paid plan
From $99/month

Model
Subscription

Works on top of
-

Difficulty
Simple - Little learning required, I am willing to learn

Website URL
https://www.sandboxcommerce.com/

Name
Apphive

Description
No code app builder

Create
Mobile Apps 📱

Free plan
-

Paid plan
From $8/month

Model
Subscription

Works on top of
-

Difficulty
Simple - Little learning required, I am willing to learn

Website URL
https://apphive.io/

Name
Outseta

Description
Payments, authentication, CRM, email—it's all here

Create
Memberships & Subscriptions 🎬

Free plan
Yes

Paid plan
From $29/month + 1% fee

Model
Subscription, Transaction-based

Works on top of
-

Difficulty
Simple - Little learning required, I am willing to learn

Website URL
https://outseta.com

Name
Stacker

Description
Build custom software that empowers your partners, teammates and customers.

Create
Internal Apps & Client Portals 💼

Free plan
-

Paid plan
From $59/month

Model
Subscription

Works on top of
Needs Airtable, Needs Google Sheets

Difficulty
Simple - Little learning required, I am willing to learn

Website URL
https://www.stackerhq.com/

Name
eDirectory

Description
Building a modern online directory and membership sites has never been easier

Create
Memberships & Subscriptions 📇, Classified Ads 🗞️, Directories 📌

Free plan
-

Paid plan
From $99/month

Model
Subscription

Works on top of
-

Difficulty
Simple - Little learning required, I am willing to learn

Website URL
https://www.edirectory.com/

Name
SheetDream

Description
Instantly build an app from your spreadsheets

Create
Communities & Forums 🗣, Directories 📌, Classified Ads 💼, Job Boards 💼, Internal Apps & Client Portals 💼, Websites ⬤

Free plan
Yes

Paid plan
From $9/month

Model
Subscription

Works on top of
Needs Airtable, Needs Google Sheets

Difficulty
I am willing to learn

Website URL
https://sheetdream.io/

Name
Linktree

Description
Connect audiences to all of your content with just one link

Create
Landing & Personal Pages 📎, Payment Pages 🖼️

Free plan
Yes

Paid plan
$6/month

Model
Subscription

Works on top of
-

Difficulty
Simple - Little learning required, I am willing to learn

Website URL
https://linktr.ee/

Name
Getform

Description
Collect payments, opinions, feedback, emails with forms available via a link

Create
Forms ❓, Landing & Personal Pages 📎

Free plan
Yes

Paid plan
From $7/month

Model
Subscription

Works on top of
-

Difficulty
Simple - Little learning required, I am willing to learn

Website URL
https://getform.com/

Name
ContactInBio

Description
Offer more contact options to your followers

Create
Landing & Personal Pages 📎, Online Stores ⬢

Free plan
Yes

Paid plan
From $4.55/month

Model
Subscription

Works on top of
-

Difficulty
Simple - Little learning required, I am willing to learn

Website URL
https://www.contactinbio.com/

Name
Campsite

Description
Your social bio link outfitter

Create
Landing & Personal Pages 📎

Free plan
Yes

Paid plan
$7/month

Model
Subscription

Works on top of
-

Difficulty
Simple - Little learning required, I am willing to learn

Website URL
https://campsite.bio/

Name
Link in Profile

Description
Drive more traffic from Instagram

Create
Landing & Personal Pages 📎

Free plan
-

Paid plan
$9.99/month

Model
Subscription

Works on top of
Needs Instagram

Difficulty
Simple - Little learning required, I am willing to learn

Website URL
https://linkinprofile.com/

Name
Linkin.bio

Description
Turn followers into customers with Linkin.bio by Later

Create
Landing & Personal Pages 🔗, Online Stores ⬢

Free plan
Yes

Paid plan
From $15/month

Model
Subscription

Works on top of
Needs Instagram

Difficulty
Simple - Little learning required, I am willing to learn

Website URL
https://later.com/linkinbio/

Name
Lnk.Bio

Description
Multiple links for your link in bio

Create
Landing & Personal Pages 📎

Free plan
Yes

Paid plan
From $0.99/month

Model
Subscription

Works on top of
-

Difficulty
Simple - Little learning required, I am willing to learn

Website URL
https://lnk.bio/

Name
Claris FileMaker

Description
An application development platform to build apps like a boss

Create
Software (Local/On-Prem) 🖥, Internal Apps & Client Portals 📇

Free plan
-

Paid plan
From $19/month

Model
Subscription, One-time payment

Works on top of
-

Difficulty
I am willing to learn

Website URL
https://www.claris.com/filemaker/

Name
Gather

Description
Make spending time with your communities just as easy as real life

Create
Virtual Spaces 🎡

Free plan
Yes

Paid plan
From $2

Model
Pay-as-you-go

Works on top of
-

Difficulty
I am willing to learn

Website URL
https://gather.town

Name
Niceboard

Description
Set up your own profitable job board in a matter of minutes

Create
Job Boards 💼

Free plan
-

Paid plan
From $129/month

Model
Subscription

Works on top of
-

Difficulty
Simple - Little learning required, I am willing to learn

Website URL
https://niceboard.co

Name
Circle

Description
Bring together your discussions, memberships, and content

Create
Memberships & Subscriptions 💵, Communities & Forums 🗣

Free plan
-

Paid plan
From $39/month

Model
Subscription

Works on top of

Difficulty
Simple - Little learning required, I am willing to learn

Website URL
circle.so

Name
Discourse

Description
Use Discourse as a mailing list, discussion forum, long-form chat room, and more

Create
Communities & Forums 🗣

Free plan
Yes

Paid plan
From $100/month

Model
Subscription

Works on top of
-

Difficulty
Simple - Little learning required, I am willing to learn

Website URL
https://www.discourse.org/

Name
OnWhats.App

Description
Create your online catalogue receive orders on WhatsApp

Create
Online Stores 🔷

Free plan
-

Paid plan
From $1/month

Model
Subscription

Works on top of
Needs WhatsApp

Difficulty
Simple - Little learning required, I am willing to learn

Website URL
https://get.onwhats.app

Name
FlutterFlow

Description
Building Flutter applications has never been easier

Create
Mobile Apps 📱

Free plan
Yes

Paid plan
From $30/month

Model
Subscription

Works on top of
-

Difficulty
Simple - Little learning required, I am willing to learn

Website URL
https://flutterflow.io

Name
Pory

Description
Build custom apps for your business without code

Create
Classified Ads 📇, Directories 📌, Memberships & Subscriptions 🎞️, Job Boards 💼

Free plan
Yes

Paid plan
From $18/month

Model
Subscription

Works on top of
Needs Airtable

Difficulty
Simple - Little learning required, I am willing to learn

Website URL
https://pory.io

Name
Sheety

Description
Turn their spreadsheets into powerful APIs to rapidly develop prototypes, websites, apps and more

Create
Mobile Apps 📱, Prototypes 💪, Websites ⚫, Directories 📌, Voting Platforms 🎲

Free plan
Yes

Paid plan
From $9.99/month

Model
Subscription

Works on top of
Needs Google Sheets

Difficulty
Simple - Little learning required, I am willing to learn

Website URL
https://sheety.co/

Name
Wappler

Description
Wappler gives you control over HTML, CSS and JavaScript but fully visually, thanks to its powerful design tools

Create
Websites 🌐, Software (Online/SaaS) 🏭, Prototypes 🤳, Mobile Apps 📱, Marketplaces 🛍, Internal Apps & Client Portals 💼, Directories 📌

Free plan
-

Paid plan
From €19/month

Model
Subscription

Works on top of
-

Difficulty
I am willing to learn

Website URL
https://wappler.io/

Name
Spread Simple

Description
A blazing-fast way to create and manage websites using Google Sheets

Create
Directories 📌, Websites 🔴, Online Stores ⬢, Classified Ads 📰, Streaming & Courses Platforms 📕, Job Boards 💼

Free plan
Yes

Paid plan
$13/month

Model
Subscription

Works on top of
Needs Google Sheets

Difficulty
Simple - Little learning required, I am willing to learn

Website URL
https://spreadsimple.com

Name
Honeycode

Description
Amazon Honeycode gives you the power to build apps for managing your team's work

Create
Internal Apps & Client Portals 💼

Free plan
Yes

Paid plan
From $19.99/month

Model
Subscription

Works on top of
-

Difficulty
Simple - Little learning required, I am willing to learn

Website URL
https://www.honeycode.aws/

Name
Teachable

Description
Transform your experience and know-how into a thriving knowledge business

Create
Streaming & Courses Platforms 🎬

Free plan
Yes

Paid plan
From $29/month

Model
Subscription

Works on top of
-

Difficulty
Simple - Little learning required, I am willing to learn

Website URL
https://teachable.com/

Name
Form to Notion

Description
Supercharge Notion with Google Forms

Create
Forms ❓

Free plan
Yes

Paid plan
Free

Model
One-time payment, Subscription, Transaction-based, Pay-as-you-go

Works on top of
Needs Notion, Needs Google Forms

Difficulty
Simple - Little learning required, I am willing to learn

Website URL
https://formtonotion.com/

Name
NotionForms

Description
Easy to use Form Builder for Notion

Create
Forms ❓

Free plan
Yes

Paid plan
$15/month

Model
Subscription

Works on top of
Needs Notion

Difficulty
Simple - Little learning required, I am willing to learn

Website URL
https://notionforms.io/

Name
Sheet Monkey

Description
Submit your forms to Google Sheets

Create
Forms ?

Free plan
Yes

Paid plan
$5/month

Model
Subscription

Works on top of
Needs Google Sheets

Difficulty
Simple - Little learning required, I am willing to learn

Website URL
https://sheetmonkey.io/

Name
Leeflets

Description
Single-page websites for all kinds of things

Create
Landing & Personal Pages 📎, Websites ⚫

Free plan
-

Paid plan
$5/month

Model
Subscription

Works on top of
-

Difficulty
Simple - Little learning required, I am willing to learn

Website URL
https://leeflets.com/

Name
Unbounce

Description
Light up new conversion possibilities for your small business

Create
Landing & Personal Pages 📎

Free plan
-

Paid plan
From $90/month

Model
Subscription

Works on top of
-

Difficulty
Simple - Little learning required, I am willing to learn

Website URL
https://unbounce.com/

Name
Launchaco

Description
The simplest way to build a website for your startup

Create
Landing & Personal Pages 📎

Free plan
Yes

Paid plan
$49.99/year

Model
Subscription

Works on top of
-

Difficulty
Simple - Little learning required, I am willing to learn

Website URL
https://www.launchaco.com/

Name
Grapedrop

Description
The best page builder for your next project

Create
Landing & Personal Pages 📎, Websites ⚫

Free plan
Yes

Paid plan
From $4.99/month

Model
Subscription

Works on top of
-

Difficulty
Simple - Little learning required, I am willing to learn

Website URL
https://grapedrop.com/

Name
Unicorn Platform

Description
Build a glorious landing page

Create
Landing & Personal Pages 📎

Free plan
Yes

Paid plan
From $8/month

Model
Subscription

Works on top of
-

Difficulty
Simple - Little learning required, I am willing to learn

Website URL
https://unicornplatform.com/

Name
Landingi

Description
The fastest, easiest way to build high-converting landing pages

Create
Landing & Personal Pages 📎

Free plan
-

Paid plan
From $55/month

Model
Subscription

Works on top of
-

Difficulty
Simple - Little learning required, I am willing to learn

Website URL
https://landingi.com/

Name
Tadabase

Description
Custom business software 10x faster

Create
Internal Apps & Client Portals 💼

Free plan
-

Paid plan
From $74/month

Model
Subscription

Works on top of
-

Difficulty
Simple - Little learning required, I am willing to learn

Website URL
https://tadabase.io/

Name
Actiondesk

Description
Easily answer questions with data

Create
Databases 📁

Free plan
-

Paid plan
From $169/month

Model
Subscription

Works on top of
-

Difficulty
Simple - Little learning required, I am willing to learn

Website URL
https://www.actiondesk.io/

Name
Stackby

Description
One tool that brings together flexibility of spreadsheets, power of databases and built-in integrations

Create
Databases 📁

Free plan
Yes

Paid plan
From $5/month

Model
Subscription

Works on top of
-

Difficulty
I am willing to learn

Website URL
https://www.stackby.com/

Name
Stein

Description
Use Google Sheets as your no-setup data store

Create
Databases 📓

Free plan
Yes

Paid plan
From $8/month

Model
Subscription

Works on top of
Needs Google Sheets

Difficulty
Simple - Little learning required, I am willing to learn

Website URL
https://steinhq.com/

Name
Grist

Description
Evolution of spreadsheets to organize your data, your way

Create
Databases 🗂

Free plan
Yes

Paid plan
From $8/month

Model
Subscription

Works on top of
-

Difficulty
Simple - Little learning required, I am willing to learn

Website URL
https://www.getgrist.com/

Name
Spider Pro

Description
The easiest way to scrape the internet

Create
Other useful tools

Free plan
-

Paid plan
$38

Model
One-time payment

Works on top of
-

Difficulty
I am willing to learn

Website URL
https://tryspider.com/

Name
Nuclino

Description
Bring all your team's knowledge, docs, and projects together in one place

Create
Documentation & Guides

Free plan
Yes

Paid plan
$5/month

Model
Subscription

Works on top of
-

Difficulty
Simple - Little learning required, I am willing to learn

Website URL
https://www.nuclino.com/

Name
Knack

Description
Quickly build business apps that get your data to the right users

Create
Internal Apps & Client Portals 💼

Free plan
-

Paid plan
From $39/mont

Model
Subscription

Works on top of
-

Difficulty
I am willing to learn

Website URL
https://www.knack.com/

Name
Databread

Description
The insights, tools, and data you need to do your job

Create
Databases 🗂

Free plan
-

Paid plan
From $10/month

Model
Subscription

Works on top of
Needs Google Chrome

Difficulty
Simple - Little learning required, I am willing to learn

Website URL
https://databread.com/

Name
Instadeq

Description
From data to insights in minutes

Create
Databases 📁

Free plan
-

Paid plan
From $30/month

Model
Subscription

Works on top of
-

Difficulty
Simple - Little learning required, I am willing to learn

Website URL
https://instadeq.com/

Name
Caspio

Description
The no-code platform for custom business applications

Create
Internal Apps & Client Portals 💼

Free plan
Yes

Paid plan
From $100/month

Model
Subscription

Works on top of
-

Difficulty
I am willing to learn

Website URL
https://www.caspio.com/

Name
FormBeaver

Description
Build database software without coding

Create
Internal Apps & Client Portals 💼, Software (Online/SaaS) 💻

Free plan
Yes

Paid plan
From $69/month

Model
Subscription

Works on top of
-

Difficulty
I am willing to learn

Website URL
https://www.formbeaver.com/

Name
Plasmic

Description
Create stunning visual content and pages

Create
Prototypes 💪

Free plan
Yes

Paid plan
From $15/month

Model
Subscription

Works on top of
-

Difficulty
I am willing to learn

Website URL
https://www.plasmic.app/

Name
Designmodo

Description
Create websites and email newsletters with our design tools

Create
Prototypes 💪, Websites ⚫, Job Boards 💼

Free plan
Yes

Paid plan
From $29/month

Model
Subscription

Works on top of
-

Difficulty
Simple - Little learning required, I am willing to learn

Website URL
https://designmodo.com/

Name
Chatfuel

Description
The easiest way to build a no-code chatbot

Create
Chatbots 💬

Free plan
Yes

Paid plan
From $15/month

Model
Subscription

Works on top of
-

Difficulty
Simple - Little learning required, I am willing to learn

Website URL
https://chatfuel.com/

Name
Voiceflow

Description
Voiceflow helps teams design, prototype and launch voice & chat assistants

Create
Chatbots 💬

Free plan
Yes

Paid plan
From $40/month

Model
Subscription

Works on top of
-

Difficulty
Simple - Little learning required, I am willing to learn

Website URL
https://www.voiceflow.com/

Name
Joonbot

Description
No-code chatbot builder

Create
Chatbots 💬

Free plan
Yes

Paid plan
From $28/month

Model
Subscription

Works on top of
-

Difficulty
Simple - Little learning required, I am willing to learn

Website URL
https://joonbot.com/

Name
ItsAlive

Description
Chatbot solutions for Facebook Messenger

Create
Chatbots 💬

Free plan
Yes

Paid plan
From $19/month

Model
Subscription

Works on top of
Needs Facebook Messenger

Difficulty
Simple - Little learning required, I am willing to learn

Website URL
https://itsalive.io/

Name
WhatsForm

Description
Get responses in WhatsApp

Create
Forms ❓

Free plan
Yes

Paid plan
$9/month

Model
Subscription

Works on top of
Needs WhatsApp

Difficulty
Simple - Little learning required, I am willing to learn

Website URL
https://whatsform.com/

Name
Landbot

Description
The most intuitive no-code chatbot builder

Create
Chatbots 💬

Free plan
Yes

Paid plan
From €30/month

Model
Subscription

Works on top of
-

Difficulty
Simple - Little learning required, I am willing to learn

Website URL
https://landbot.io/

Name
Chatamo

Description
The world's easiest bot creator for small organisations

Create
Chatbots 💬

Free plan
Yes

Paid plan
From £49/month

Model
Subscription

Works on top of
-

Difficulty
Simple - Little learning required, I am willing to learn

Website URL
https://chatamo.com/

Name
Crisp

Description
Give your customer experience a human touch

Create
Chatbots 💬

Free plan
Yes

Paid plan
From €25/month

Model
Subscription

Works on top of
-

Difficulty
Simple - Little learning required, I am willing to learn

Website URL
https://crisp.chat/

Name
Backendless

Description
Complete visual app builder that makes apps intuitive to develop and easy to manage

Create
Internal Apps & Client Portals 💼

Free plan
Yes

Paid plan
From $25/month

Model
Subscription

Works on top of
-

Difficulty
I am willing to learn

Website URL
https://backendless.com/

Name
Kreezalid

Description
Create and grow your custom online marketplace

Create
Marketplaces 🎭

Free plan
-

Paid plan
$299/month

Model
Subscription

Works on top of
-

Difficulty
Simple - Little learning required, I am willing to learn

Website URL
https://www.kreezalid.com/

Name
Clappia

Description
Let anyone in your business build mobile & web apps

Create
Internal Apps & Client Portals 💼

Free plan
-

Paid plan
From $4/month

Model
Subscription

Works on top of
-

Difficulty
Simple - Little learning required, I am willing to learn

Website URL
https://www.clappia.com/

Name
DronaHQ

Description
Build stunning internal tools, blazing fast

Create
Internal Apps & Client Portals 💼

Free plan
-

Paid plan
From $100/month

Model
Subscription

Works on top of
-

Difficulty
I am willing to learn

Website URL
https://www.dronahq.com/

Name
Qalcwise

Description
Build your custom app or buy ready-made one

Create
Internal Apps & Client Portals 💼

Free plan
Yes

Paid plan
From €10/month

Model
Subscription

Works on top of
-

Difficulty
I am willing to learn

Website URL
https://qalcwise.com/

Name
Quixy

Description
Businesses need digital solutions Fast

Create
Internal Apps & Client Portals 💼

Free plan
-

Paid plan
From $18/month

Model
Subscription

Works on top of
-

Difficulty
I am willing to learn

Website URL
https://quixy.com/

Name
Jungleworks

Description
Create an online marketplace

Create
Marketplaces 👥

Free plan
-

Paid plan
From $49/month

Model
Subscription

Works on top of
-

Difficulty
I am willing to learn

Website URL
https://jungleworks.com/

Name
UserGuiding

Description
Boost your growth in a couple of clicks with onboarding flows

Create
Documentation & Guides

Free plan
-

Paid plan
From $99/mont

Model
Subscription

Works on top of
-

Difficulty
I am willing to learn

Website URL
https://userguiding.com/

Name
KgBase

Description
Build no-code knowledge graphs with KgBase

Create
Documentation & Guides 🗂, *Other useful tools*

Free plan
-

Paid plan
From $19/month

Model
Subscription

Works on top of
-

Difficulty
Simple - Little learning required, I am willing to learn

Website URL
https://www.kgbase.com/

Name
GW Apps

Description
Easily build apps and digitize your business

Create
Internal Apps & Client Portals 💼

Free plan
-

Paid plan
From $5/month

Model
Subscription

Works on top of
-

Difficulty
Simple - Little learning required, I am willing to learn

Website URL
https://gwapps.com/

Name
Spreadsheet.com

Description
One familiar tool with the power of a database and project management system

Create
Databases 📁, Internal Apps & Client Portals 📁

Free plan
Yes

Paid plan
From $9/month

Model
Subscription

Works on top of
-

Difficulty
I am willing to learn

Website URL
https://www.spreadsheet.com/

Name
Molnify

Description
Start from a template, modify it and make it your own app

Create
Software (Local/On-Prem) 🖥, Internal Apps & Client Portals 💼, Mobile Apps 📱

Free plan
Yes

Paid plan
From $230/month

Model
Subscription

Works on top of
Needs Microsoft Excel, Needs Google Sheets

Difficulty
Simple - Little learning required, I am willing to learn

Website URL
https://www.molnify.com/

Name
Open as App

Description
Automatic app creation for every spreadsheet user

Create
Internal Apps & Client Portals 💼

Free plan
Yes

Paid plan
From $90/month

Model
Subscription

Works on top of
Needs Google Sheets, Needs Microsoft Excel

Difficulty
Simple - Little learning required, I am willing to learn

Website URL
https://www.openasapp.com/

Name
Buildbox

Description
Create 3D & 2D video games without coding

Create
Video Games 🎮

Free plan
Yes

Paid plan
From $19.99/month

Model
Subscription

Works on top of
-

Difficulty
I am willing to learn

Website URL
https://signup.buildbox.com/

Name
Kodika

Description
A no code iOS app maker that simplifies mobile app development

Create
Mobile Apps 📱

Free plan
Yes

Paid plan
$24.99/month

Model
Subscription

Works on top of
-

Difficulty
I am willing to learn

Website URL
https://kodika.io/

Name
AppMachine

Description
AppMachine enables anyone to make apps

Create
Mobile Apps 📱

Free plan
-

Paid plan
From $49/month

Model
Subscription

Works on top of
-

Difficulty
I am willing to learn

Website URL
https://www.appmachine.com/

Name
BuildFire

Description
Powerful and easy to use mobile app builder

Create
Mobile Apps 📱

Free plan
-

Paid plan
From $159/month

Model
Subscription

Works on top of
-

Difficulty
I am willing to learn

Website URL
https://buildfire.com/

Name
AppStylo

Description
Best mobile app maker for your business

Create
Mobile Apps 📱

Free plan
-

Paid plan
From $14/month

Model
Subscription

Works on top of
-

Difficulty
Simple - Little learning required, I am willing to learn

Website URL
https://appstylo.com/

Name
Fliplet

Description
Prefab: The smart way to create custom apps

Create
Mobile Apps 📱

Free plan
Yes

Paid plan
From $9.90/month

Model
Subscription

Works on top of
-

Difficulty
I am willing to learn

Website URL
https://fliplet.com/

Name
Snappii

Description
Apps in a snap

Create
Mobile Apps 📱, Internal Apps & Client Portals 💼

Free plan
-

Paid plan
From $20/month

Model
Subscription

Works on top of
-

Difficulty
Simple - Little learning required, I am willing to learn

Website URL
https://www.snappii.com/

Name
Clarifai

Description
The fastest way to transform your unstructured image, video, text, and audio data into actionable insights

Create
AI Tools 🤖, Internal Apps & Client Portals 💼

Free plan
Yes

Paid plan
From $30/month

Model
Subscription

Works on top of
-

Difficulty
I am willing to learn

Website URL
https://www.clarifai.com/

Name
Pirsch

Description
Simple, privacy-friendly, open-source alternative to Google Analytics

Create
Website Activity Trackers

Free plan
-

Paid plan
From $4/month

Model
Subscription

Works on top of
-

Difficulty
Simple - Little learning required, I am willing to learn

Website URL
https://pirsch.io/

Name
Magic

Description
Get peace of mind with secure, extensible passwordless authentication that's built to scale

Create
Authentication & ID Verification 🔐

Free plan
-

Paid plan
From $0.034/month

Model
Pay-as-you-go

Works on top of
-

Difficulty
Simple - Little learning required, I am willing to learn

Website URL
https://magic.link/

Name
Provenly

Description
Skyrocket conversions by over 250% in just a 5 minutes

Create
Testimonial Pages 🖤

Free plan
Yes

Paid plan
From $99

Model
One-time payment

Works on top of
-

Difficulty
Simple - Little learning required, I am willing to learn

Website URL
https://proven.ly/

Name
Leadpages

Description
Turn clicks into customers

Create
Landing & Personal Pages 📎

Free plan
-

Paid plan
From $27/month

Model
Subscription

Works on top of
-

Difficulty
Simple - Little learning required, I am willing to learn

Website URL
https://www.leadpages.com/

Name
Commotion

Description
Create forms, embed them anywhere, and save responses to a Notion page

Create
Forms ?

Free plan
Yes

Paid plan
$10/month

Model
Subscription

Works on top of
Needs Notion

Difficulty
Simple - Little learning required, I am willing to learn

Website URL
https://commotion.page/

Name
WeWeb

Description
Build custom web applications powered by your data

Create
Classified Ads, Directories, Online Stores, Marketplaces, Internal Apps & Client Portals, Software (Online/SaaS), Communities & Forums, Job Boards

Free plan
Yes

Paid plan
From $35/month

Model
Subscription

Works on top of
-

Difficulty
I am willing to learn

Website URL
https://www.weweb.io/

Name
Fruition

Description
Free, open source toolkit for building websites with Notion

Create
Websites 🔘, Directories 📌, Landing & Personal Pages 📎

Free plan
Yes

Paid plan
Free

Model
One-time payment, Subscription, Transaction-based, Pay-as-you-go

Works on top of
Needs Notion

Difficulty
I am willing to learn

Website URL
https://fruitionsite.com/

Name
Luma

Description
Foster meaningful relationships with events, newsletters, and community analytics

Create
Communities & Forums 🗣, Virtual Events ⛺

Free plan
Yes

Paid plan
$39/month

Model
Subscription

Works on top of
-

Difficulty
Simple - Little learning required, I am willing to learn

Website URL
https://lu.ma/

Name
Kommunity

Description
All-in-One platform to easily manage your community and organize virtual, hybrid or in-person events

Create
Communities & Forums 🗣, Virtual Events ⛺

Free plan
Yes

Paid plan
From $7.99/month

Model
Subscription

Works on top of
-

Difficulty
Simple - Little learning required, I am willing to learn

Website URL
https://kommunity.com/

Name
Cotter

Description
No-code passwordless login for your website

Create
Authentication & ID Verification 🔐

Free plan
-

Paid plan
From $30/month

Model
Subscription

Works on top of
-

Difficulty
Simple - Little learning required, I am willing to learn

Website URL
https://www.cotter.app/

Name
Google Custom Search Engine

Description
Add a customizable search box to your web pages and show fast, relevant results powered by Google

Create
Search Engines & Tools 🔍

Free plan
Yes

Paid plan
Depends

Model
One-time payment, Subscription, Transaction-based, Pay-as-you-go

Works on top of
-

Difficulty
Simple - Little learning required, I am willing to learn

Website URL
https://cse.google.com

Name
Makeswift

Description
The multiplayer website builder you've been looking for

Create
Websites 🌐, Landing & Personal Pages 📎

Free plan
Yes

Paid plan
$15/month

Model
Subscription

Works on top of
-

Difficulty
Simple - Little learning required, I am willing to learn

Website URL
https://www.makeswift.com/

Name
Reform

Description
Putting together clean, on-brand forms for your business should be easy

Create
Forms ?

Free plan
-

Paid plan
$119/year

Model
Subscription

Works on top of
-

Difficulty
Simple - Little learning required, I am willing to learn

Website URL
https://www.reform.app/

Name
Workflows by Anvil

Description
Replace your paperwork with a simple, intuitive, and secure online workflow that auto-fills your forms

Create
Automations & APIs

Free plan
Yes

Paid plan
From $10/month

Model
Subscription

Works on top of
-

Difficulty
I am willing to learn

Website URL
https://www.useanvil.com/products/workflows/

Name
Nebo

Description
Make any React website no-code

Create
Prototypes 💪

Free plan
Yes

Paid plan
From $15/month

Model
Subscription

Works on top of
-

Difficulty
I am willing to learn

Website URL
https://nebohq.com/

Name
MyTemplate

Description
A no-code personal website builder for developers

Create
Landing & Personal Pages 📎

Free plan
Yes

Paid plan
Free

Model
One-time payment, Subscription, Transaction-based, Pay-as-you-go

Works on top of
-

Difficulty
I am willing to learn

Website URL
https://mytemplate.xyz/

Name
FromNotion

Description
A web app to build your landing pages on top of Notion

Create
Landing & Personal Pages 📎

Free plan
-

Paid plan
From $8/month

Model
Subscription

Works on top of
Needs Notion

Difficulty
Simple - Little learning required, I am willing to learn

Website URL
https://fromnotion.com/

Name
Jestor

Description
No-code internal tool builder to scale startup operations

Create
Internal Apps & Client Portals 💼

Free plan
Yes

Paid plan
From $9/month

Model
Subscription

Works on top of
-

Difficulty
I am willing to learn

Website URL
https://jestor.com/

Name
GingerTag

Description
Simple, no-code, privacy friendly analytics

Create
Website Activity Trackers

Free plan
Yes

Paid plan
From $10/month

Model
Subscription

Works on top of
-

Difficulty
Simple - Little learning required, I am willing to learn

Website URL
https://gingertag.com/

Name
Friendly

Description
The most popular Swiss Google Analytics alternative

Create
Website Activity Trackers

Free plan
-

Paid plan
From €49/month

Model
Subscription

Works on top of
-

Difficulty
Simple - Little learning required, I am willing to learn

Website URL
https://friendly.ch/

Name
Edition

Description
No-code publishing platform with the ease of Notion

Create
Communities & Forums 🗣, Documentation & Guides 💼, Internal Apps & Client Portals 🗳, Voting Platforms 📦

Free plan
Yes

Paid plan
From $12/month

Model
Subscription

Works on top of
-

Difficulty
Simple - Little learning required, I am willing to learn

Website URL
https://edition.so/

Name
Silex

Description
Open source website builder - no-code for designers & makers

Create
Websites 🌐

Free plan
Yes

Paid plan
Free

Model
One-time payment, Subscription, Transaction-based, Pay-as-you-go

Works on top of
-

Difficulty
I am willing to learn

Website URL
https://www.silex.me/

Name
Fireapis

Description
Build APIs with no-code

Create
Automations & APIs

Free plan
Yes

Paid plan
From $15/month

Model
Subscription

Works on top of
-

Difficulty
I am willing to learn

Website URL
https://fireapis.com/

Name
Teyuto

Description
Create your customized video platform

Create
Streaming & Courses Platforms

Free plan
-

Paid plan
From $99/month

Model
Subscription

Works on top of

Difficulty
I am willing to learn

Website URL
https://teyuto.com

Name
Guestboard

Description
From camping trips to conferences, Guestboard is the fastest way to turn any event into an engaged, short-term community

Create
Communities & Forums 🗣, Virtual Events ⛺

Free plan
Yes

Paid plan
From $1

Model
Pay-as-you-go

Works on top of
-

Difficulty
Simple - Little learning required, I am willing to learn

Website URL
https://guestboard.co

Name
OnlyDomains

Description
Everything you need to get online

Create
Websites

Free plan
-

Paid plan
From €3.89/month

Model
Subscription

Works on top of
-

Difficulty
I am willing to learn

Website URL
https://www.onlydomains.com

Name
PeerBoard

Description
Embed a community into any website

Create
Communities & Forums 🗣

Free plan
Yes

Paid plan
From $29/month

Model
Subscription

Works on top of
-

Difficulty
Simple - Little learning required, I am willing to learn

Website URL
https://peerboard.com/

Name
Spore

Description
A free, all-in-one website builder for creators

Create
Communities & Forums 🗣, Memberships & Subscriptions 🎞

Free plan
Yes

Paid plan
Free

Model
One-time payment, Subscription, Transaction-based, Pay-as-you-go

Works on top of
-

Difficulty
Simple - Little learning required, I am willing to learn

Website URL
https://spore.build/

Name
OnlyFams

Description
Create private communities for your fams

Create
Communities & Forums 🗣, Memberships & Subscriptions 🎞

Free plan
Yes

Paid plan
From $30/month

Model
Subscription

Works on top of
-

Difficulty
Simple - Little learning required, I am willing to learn

Website URL
https://www.onlyfams.co/

Name
Tribe

Description
A customizable community platform for businesses

Create
Communities & Forums

Free plan
Yes

Paid plan
From $49/month

Model
Subscription

Works on top of
-

Difficulty
Simple - Little learning required, I am willing to learn

Website URL
https://tribe.so/

Name
Matomo

Description
Google Analytics alternative that protects your data and your customers' privacy

Create
Website Activity Trackers

Free plan
Yes

Paid plan
From €29/month

Model
Subscription

Works on top of
-

Difficulty
Simple - Little learning required, I am willing to learn

Website URL
https://matomo.org/

Name
Zappter

Description
Create your own app with drag and drop and zero code

Create
Mobile Apps 📱

Free plan
Yes

Paid plan
From $9.90/month

Model
Subscription

Works on top of
-

Difficulty
Simple - Little learning required, I am willing to learn

Website URL
https://www.zappter.com/

Name
BlockSurvey

Description
BlockSurvey is an end-to-end encrypted survey tool, helping people collect sensitive data

Create
Forms ❓

Free plan
-

Paid plan
From $8/month

Model
Subscription

Works on top of
-

Difficulty
I am willing to learn

Website URL
https://blocksurvey.io/

Name
Straw.Page

Description
Straw.Page lets you create unique websites straight from your phone

Create
Websites 🌐, Landing & Personal Pages 📎, Online Stores ⬢

Free plan
Yes

Paid plan
$49/year

Model
Subscription

Works on top of
-

Difficulty
Simple - Little learning required, I am willing to learn

Website URL
https://straw.page/

Name
Cloakist

Description
Put Airtable forms, ClickUp documents, Adobe Spark pages, Trello boards and more at your custom domain, with your branding

Create
Websites 🌑

Free plan
-

Paid plan
From $10/month

Model
Subscription

Works on top of
-

Difficulty
Simple - Little learning required, I am willing to learn

Website URL
https://cloak.ist/

Name
Interactive Calculators

Description
User friendly website calculators

Create
Calculators 🧮

Free plan
Yes

Paid plan
$19/month

Model
Subscription

Works on top of
-

Difficulty
Simple - Little learning required, I am willing to learn

Website URL
https://www.interactivecalculator.com/

Name
Calconic

Description
Build your web calculator using our simple drag-and-drop editor

Create
Calculators 🧾

Free plan
Yes

Paid plan
From €4/month

Model
Subscription

Works on top of
-

Difficulty
Simple - Little learning required, I am willing to learn

Website URL
https://www.calconic.com/

Name
Datawrapper

Description
Enrich your stories with charts, maps, and tables

Create
Charts & Maps

Free plan
Yes

Paid plan
$599/month

Model
Subscription

Works on top of
-

Difficulty
Simple - Little learning required, I am willing to learn

Website URL
https://www.datawrapper.de/

Name
Noloco

Description
Build the perfect app for your business

Create
Internal Apps & Client Portals 💼

Free plan
-

Paid plan
From $55/month

Model
Subscription

Works on top of
Needs Airtable, Needs Google Sheets

Difficulty
Simple - Little learning required, I am willing to learn

Website URL
https://noloco.io/

Name
Wized

Description
Rapidly build real web applications without coding

Create
Memberships & Subscriptions , Internal Apps & Client Portals , Software (Online/SaaS) , Streaming & Courses Platforms

Free plan
Yes

Paid plan
From $19/month

Model
Subscription

Works on top of
Needs Webflow

Difficulty
I am willing to learn

Website URL
https://www.wized.io/

Name
Graphite

Description
Create live websites just like in a graphic editor

Create
Websites 💪, Prototypes 💪, Landing & Personal Pages 📎

Free plan
Yes

Paid plan
Free

Model
One-time payment, Subscription, Transaction-based, Pay-as-you-go

Works on top of
-

Difficulty
Simple - Little learning required, I am willing to learn

Website URL
https://graphite.space/

Name
Blocs

Description
The ultimate Mac website builder

Create
Websites ⚫

Free plan
-

Paid plan
From $99.99

Model
One-time payment

Works on top of
-

Difficulty
I am willing to learn

Website URL
https://blocsapp.com/

Name
Airvues

Description
The fast and easy way to build web apps using Airtable without writing code

Create
Blogs 📓, Directories 📌, Job Boards 💼, Landing & Personal Pages 📎, Classified Ads 📕, Websites ⚫, Software (Online/SaaS) 🎓

Free plan
Yes

Paid plan
From $5/month

Model
Subscription

Works on top of
Needs Airtable

Difficulty
Simple - Little learning required, I am willing to learn

Website URL
https://airvues.com/

Name
Notelet

Description
Create a website or blog with Notion

Create
Landing & Personal Pages 🔖, Blogs 📰, Websites ⚫

Free plan
Yes

Paid plan
$7/month

Model
Subscription

Works on top of
Needs Notion

Difficulty
Simple - Little learning required, I am willing to learn

Website URL
https://notelet.so/

Name
Swipe Pages

Description
Build high converting landing pages in minutes

Create
Landing & Personal Pages 📎

Free plan
-

Paid plan
From $29/month

Model
Subscription

Works on top of
-

Difficulty
Simple - Little learning required, I am willing to learn

Website URL
https://swipepages.com/

Name
Parabola

Description
Parabola is the home base for teams to collaboratively document and automate everyday processes

Create
Automations & APIs

Free plan
Yes

Paid plan
From $80/month

Model
Subscription

Works on top of
-

Difficulty
I am willing to learn

Website URL
https://parabola.io/

Name
Paytable

Description
Deliver Airtable, Notion + more securely to your audience in seconds

Create
Memberships & Subscriptions 🎞

Free plan
Yes

Paid plan
From $10/month

Model
Subscription

Works on top of
Needs Airtable, Needs Notion, Needs Google Sheets

Difficulty
Simple - Little learning required, I am willing to learn

Website URL
https://paytable.io/

Name
the:gist

Description
The easiest way to automate your Notion workflows

Create
Automations & APIs

Free plan
Yes

Paid plan
From $5/month

Model
Subscription

Works on top of
Needs Notion

Difficulty
Simple - Little learning required, I am willing to learn

Website URL
https://www.thegist.so/

Name
Popsy

Description
Create websites from Notion for free

Create
Websites

Free plan
Yes

Paid plan
Free

Model
One-time payment, Subscription, Transaction-based, Pay-as-you-go

Works on top of
Needs Notion

Difficulty
Simple - Little learning required, I am willing to learn

Website URL
https://popsy.co/

Name
Levity

Description
Create your own AI for documents, images, or text that takes daily, repetitive tasks off your shoulders

Create
AI Tools 🤖, Internal Apps & Client Portals 💼

Free plan
-

Paid plan
Pay-as-you-go (min $100/month)

Model
Subscription, Pay-as-you-go

Works on top of
-

Difficulty
I am willing to learn

Website URL
https://levity.ai/

Name
Payhip

Description
Payhip is the easiest way to sell digital downloads & memberships

Create
Online Stores 🔷, Memberships & Subscriptions 🎞️

Free plan
Yes

Paid plan
From $30/month + 2% transaction fee

Model
Subscription, Transaction-based

Works on top of
-

Difficulty
Simple - Little learning required, I am willing to learn

Website URL
https://payhip.com/

Name
Sellfy

Description
Sell your products hassle-free

Create
Online Stores ⬢

Free plan
Yes

Paid plan
From $19/month

Model
Subscription

Works on top of

Difficulty
Simple - Little learning required, I am willing to learn

Website URL
https://sellfy.com/

Name
BigCommerce

Description
Selling made simple

Create
Online Stores

Free plan
-

Paid plan
From 29.95/month

Model
Subscription

Works on top of
-

Difficulty
Simple - Little learning required, I am willing to learn

Website URL
https://www.bigcommerce.com/essentials/

Name
SendOwl

Description
The wise way to sell your digital products

Create
Online Stores

Free plan
-

Paid plan
From $15/month

Model
Subscription

Works on top of
-

Difficulty
Simple - Little learning required, I am willing to learn

Website URL
https://www.sendowl.com/

Name
DPD

Description
Sell and deliver your ebooks and downloads

Create
Online Stores

Free plan
-

Paid plan
From $10/month

Model
Subscription

Works on top of
-

Difficulty
Simple - Little learning required, I am willing to learn

Website URL
https://getdpd.com/

Name
Easy Digital Downloads

Description
Sell digital product with WordPress

Create
Online Stores

Free plan
-

Paid plan
From $199/year

Model
Subscription

Works on top of
Needs WordPress

Difficulty
I am willing to learn

Website URL
https://easydigitaldownloads.com/

Name
MemberPress

Description
The all-in-one membership plugin for WordPress

Create
Memberships & Subscriptions 🎞️

Free plan
-

Paid plan
From $279/year

Model
Subscription

Works on top of
Needs WordPress

Difficulty
I am willing to learn

Website URL
https://memberpress.com/

Name
Calendly

Description
Easy scheduling ahead

Create
Booking Platforms 📇

Free plan
Yes

Paid plan
From $8/month

Model
Subscription

Works on top of
-

Difficulty
Simple - Little learning required, I am willing to learn

Website URL
https://calendly.com/en

Name
Beyonk

Description
Bookings made easy

Create
Booking Platforms 📖

Free plan

Paid plan
Pay-as-you-go

Model
Pay-as-you-go

Works on top of
-

Difficulty
Simple - Little learning required, I am willing to learn

Website URL
https://beyonk.com/

Name
SimplyBook.me

Description
Online booking system for all service based industries

Create
Booking Platforms 📓

Free plan
-

Paid plan
From €6.7/month

Model
Subscription

Works on top of
-

Difficulty
Simple - Little learning required, I am willing to learn

Website URL
https://simplybook.me/en/

Name
Tendeta

Description
Turn your Airtable into an ecommerce

Create
Online Stores

Free plan
Yes

Paid plan
From €9/month

Model
Subscription

Works on top of
Needs Airtable

Difficulty
Simple - Little learning required

Website URL
https://tendeta.io/

Name
AppMaster

Description
No coding skills are required to create a unique app ecosystem using only AppMaster

Create
Internal Apps & Client Portals 💼, Mobile Apps 📱

Free plan
-

Paid plan
From $5/month

Model
Subscription

Works on top of
-

Difficulty
Simple - Little learning required

Website URL
https://appmaster.io/

Name
Staticblocks

Description
A drag and drop static responsive one-page website builder

Create
Landing & Personal Pages 🔖, Websites ⬤

Free plan
Yes

Paid plan
From $49/year

Model
Subscription

Works on top of
-

Difficulty
Simple - Little learning required

Website URL
https://staticblocks.com/

Name
Jet Admin

Description
Build business apps fast and with No-Code

Create
Internal Apps & Client Portals

Free plan
Yes

Paid plan
From $24/month

Model
Subscription

Works on top of
-

Difficulty
Simple - Little learning required

Website URL
https://www.jetadmin.io/

Name
SAWO Passwordless Authentication

Description
Enable passwordless auth and drive conversions on Bubble

Create
Authentication & ID Verification

Free plan
Yes

Paid plan
Free

Model
One-time payment

Works on top of
Needs Bubble

Difficulty
I am willing to learn

Website URL
https://bubble.sawolabs.com/

Name
Candu

Description
No-code UI component builder for SaaS products

Create
Documentation & Guides 📚, Landing & Personal Pages 🔗, Internal Apps & Client Portals 💼

Free plan
Yes

Paid plan
From $49/month

Model
Subscription

Works on top of
-

Difficulty
Simple - Little learning required

Website URL
https://www.candu.ai/

Name
Simple.ink

Description
Build websites with Notion in ~10 sec

Create
Websites 🌐, Landing & Personal Pages 📎, Online Stores 🔷, Job Boards 💼

Free plan
Yes

Paid plan
From $12/month

Model
Subscription

Works on top of
Needs Notion

Difficulty
Simple - Little learning required

Website URL
https://www.simple.ink/

Name
InviteMember

Description
InviteMember makes it simple to start a paid subscription service in Telegram

Create
Memberships & Subscriptions 🎬

Free plan
Yes

Paid plan
From $0 + 10% / $49/month + 3%

Model
Subscription, Pay-as-you-go

Works on top of
Needs Telegram

Difficulty
Simple - Little learning required

Website URL
https://invitemember.com/

Name
TGmembership

Description
Fully automated, customisable paid Telegram membership bot

Create
Memberships & Subscriptions

Free plan
Yes

Paid plan
From $0 + 7% / €35/month

Model
Subscription, Pay-as-you-go

Works on top of
Needs Telegram

Difficulty
Simple - Little learning required

Website URL
https://tgmembership.com/

Name
BOWWE

Description
Create unique website designs in a powerful drag & drop builder

Create
Websites 🌐, Landing & Personal Pages 📎

Free plan
Yes

Paid plan
From $5/month

Model
Subscription, One-time payment

Works on top of
-

Difficulty
Simple - Little learning required

Website URL
https://bowwe.com/en/

Name
DataMaker21

Description
Test data generator. Make mock (aka synthetic) data for free.

Create
Other useful tools

Free plan
Yes

Paid plan
Free

Model
One-time payment, Subscription

Works on top of
-

Difficulty
Simple - Little learning required

Website URL
https://www.data21.io/datamaker21/

Name
Really Simple Support

Description
Really Simple Support is an effective, no-code solution for your product's customer support needs

Create
Documentation & Guides 📚, *Other useful tools* 💡

Free plan
Yes

Paid plan
$8/month

Model
Subscription

Works on top of
-

Difficulty
Simple - Little learning required

Website URL
https://reallysimplesupport.com/

Name
Voltapp

Description
Nocode empowerment now scalable

Create
Forms ❓, Internal Apps & Client Portals 🗃️, Marketplaces 🛍️, Virtual Events 🎪

Free plan
-

Paid plan
$119/month

Model
Subscription

Works on top of
Needs Airtable

Difficulty
I am willing to learn

Website URL
https://www.voltapp.tech/

Name
No Code Map App

Description
The easiest way to build custom interactive maps with dynamic filters

Create
Charts & Maps

Free plan
Yes

Paid plan
From $15/month

Model
Subscription, Pay-as-you-go

Works on top of
-

Difficulty
Simple - Little learning required

Website URL
https://www.nocodemapapp.com/

Name
Cogniflow

Description
AI made easy. Automate and create with the power of AI. Build and use AI without a single line of code.

Create
Charts & Maps

Free plan
Yes

Paid plan
From $50/month

Model
Subscription

Works on top of
-

Difficulty
Simple - Little learning required

Website URL
https://www.cogniflow.ai/

Index

AI Tools *209, 260, 285*

Authentication & ID Verification *37, 95, 221, 220*

Automation & APIs *25-30, 37, 38, 53, 224, 233, 256, 258, 275*

Blogs *13, 33, 34, 64, 68, 72, 74, 75, 77, 100, 103, 104, 116, 117, 253, 254*

Booking Platforms *10, 53, 268-270*

Calculators *122, 246, 247*

Charts & Maps *248, 284*

Chatbots *181-184, 186-188*

Classified Ads *10, 16, 34, 90, 119, 135, 136, 151, 155, 215, 253*

Communities & Forums *10, 34, 136, 147, 148, 215, 218, 219, 231, 235, 237, 238, 239, 240*

Databases *12, 43, 168-171, 175, 176, 199*

Directories *16, 34, 90, 119, 135, 136, 151, 152, 153, 155, 215, 217, 253*

Documentation & Guides *13, 125, 173, 196, 197, 231, 276, 276, 280*

Forms *41, 42, 45, 56, 60, 65, 66, 113, 138, 158, 159, 160, 185, 214, 223, 243, 283*

Internal Apps & Client Portals *10, 24, 34, 46, 71, 90, 90, 98, 134, 136, 144, 153, 156, 167, 174, 177, 178, 189, 191-194, 198-201, 208, 209, 215, 228, 231, 249, 260, 272, 274, 276, 283*

Job Boards *10, 16, 34, 90, 119, 136, 146, 151, 153, 180, 215, 253, 277*

Landing & Personal Pages *17, 33, 62, 72, 77, 88, 94, 96, 99, 105, 109, 114, 115, 117, 137-143, 161-166, 213, 217, 222, 226, 227, 244, 250, 251, 253-255, 273, 276, 277, 280*

Marketplaces *10, 16, 34, 90, 110, 153, 190, 195, 215, 280*

Memberships & Subscriptions *10, 16, 34, 37, 38, 77, 78, 79, 80, 107, 108, 126, 133, 135, 147, 151, 238, 239, 250, 257, 261, 267, 278, 279*

Messaging Apps *10, 34*

Mobile Apps *10, 14, 15, 24, 36, 38, 44, 48, 71, 88, 111, 122-124,*

128-132, 152, 153, 200, 203-208, 242, 272, 277

Online Stores *18, 33, 34, 39, 58, 59, 72, 77, 86, 92, 96, 101, 102, 103, 106, 107, 111, 113, 116, 119, 120, 131, 139, 149, 150, 151, 153, 244, 261-266, 271*

Payment Pages *31, 32, 37, 39, 61, 63, 137*

Pricing Pages *19*

Prototypes *10, 44, 47, 48, 81-84, 87, 97, 112, 152, 153, 179, 180, 225, 251*

Search Engines & Tools *34, 221*

Software (Local/On-Prem) *144, 200*

Software (Online/SaaS) *10, 14, 16, 16, 24, 34, 90, 153, 176, 215, 250, 253*

Streaming & Courses Platforms *10, 34, 107, 155, 157, 234, 250*

Testimonial Pages *67, 212*

Translations *40*

Video Games *202*

Virtual Events *218, 219, 235, 280*

Virtual Spaces *27, 145*

Voting Platforms *10, 16, 34, 119, 152, 231*

Website Activity Trackers *20, 21, 23, 210, 229, 230, 241*

Websites *10, 16-18, 22, 33, 34, 38, 62, 72, 76, 77, 77, 85, 88, 89, 90, 92, 93, 96, 97, 99, 101, 102, 103, 105-107, 109, 111-113, 115-120, 222, 232, 236, 244, 245, 251-254, 289, 173, 273, 277, 280*

Additional resources

No code resources

Doc Williams on YouTube - Business development made easy
https://www.youtube.com/channel/UCXv_CS0DaUVS25tFGkRALoA

NoCodeJournal - News, trends on no-code and low code
https://www.nocodejournal.com/

No code communities

Makerpad - Build your ideas, no code required
https://www.makerpad.co/

Nucode - No code maker community

290

You are the maker of a no code tool and you would like to share it with people who want to build an app, a website, a SaaS and more without coding?

Contribute to the no code movement and submit your tool! Drop us a message with the name of your tool, a short description, the website URL and your contact details. We will review your submission and get back to you!

lxvolition(at)pm.me

Scan this QR code and access the table
with all the tools (in Airtable)

Printed in France by Amazon
Brétigny-sur-Orge, FR